Nude Truths

An Odyssey in Poetry, Painting, and Prose

This publication was issued in conjunction with the publication of *Everything Must Change: Jesus, Global Crises, and a Revolution of Hope* by Brian D. McLaren and subsequent Tour 2008.

Quotations by Denise Levertov are reprinted by permission of New Directions Publishing Corp. Sales Territory: U.S./Canada rights only.

Cover image taken from Painting #6, Pilgrim Sandals. Cover design by Mary Ylvisaker Nilsen.

ISBN 978-0-9627147-5-7

Zion Publishing
1500 Crown Colony Ct. #540
Des Moines, IA 50315-1073

www.zionpublishing.org

1-800-996-2777

Printed in China
Sure Print & Design

Foreword

I stood in the gallery, staring at the exhibit—24 large, black-framed paintings, the colors descending into darks and then back out into lights. "You must be so proud," a friend said. But what I felt was humble gratitude for having had the privilege of being, in a sense, a surrogate mother. The spirit of creativity has always had a way of finding receptive wombs and then birthing into the world what needs to be birthed.

I remembered the moment of conception. It came in a dream. Or was it a vision? A visitation?

I entered into a space lush with old, beautiful furniture, woven things, pottery, art, plants hanging from macramé hangers against the window at the far end, the air steeped in smells of fresh bread and coffee. Then, against the window, I saw a woman's form approaching me. As she came closer, she said, "Are you Mary Nilsen?" I said, "Yes," and her eyes met mine for one crucial moment as she said, "I've been wanting to meet you. My name is Denise Levertov." She took my right hand and put her left arm over my shoulder and said something into my ear.

Then I awoke, pulled out of that space between sleep and consciousness, that liminal space described in Celtic spirituality as "thin space"—a place where, for any reason, the veil between oneself and the divine thins. Lying on my bed, recalling every color, every texture, every smell, I realized, suddenly, that I could not remember what she had said to me. I knew it was profoundly important, but I had no idea what it was.

Then came the real shocker. A couple of weeks later, I read in *Time* magazine that Denise Levertov had died December 20, 1997, the very night of my dream.

Could her spirit have spoken to me as she passed through the veil to the other side? And if so, what did she say? The lost words haunted me. How could I have forgotten them!

Fast forward six years to New Year's Eve 2003. The family had gathered in California for a wedding. My sister Kristi, an artist who lives in Norway, said to me early that morning, "Mary, we should do a project together." Without my willing it so, her words moved into that thin space where inspiration can happen.

The next day, after seeing a movie that commented at length on the difference between naked and nude, I said in a flash, "The title of our exhibit has to be 'Nude Truths.'" "What?" "You know, the art show you suggested, 'Nude Truths,'—naked truths presented in a beautiful, artful way, so they are nude, not naked." "Hmmmm," she said, and I knew those words were going into a place, deep in her gut, where she ruminates—her form of thin space. The next morning I awoke with another flash of inspiration, rushed into Kristi's room, and said, "We have to use the words of Denise Levertov!"

From that point on, the project was out of our hands. Denise led us "deeper into our labyrinth of valleys and mountains," as she wrote in "Her Name is Proverb."

I read everything I could find about Levertov's life. Her ideals, her passions, her vision resonated within me. Then I began reading her poetry. The deep truths and inspired pulse of her writing sent a charge through me that left me at times shaking and at other times weeping. As I read, I looked for lines that were evocative, lines I thought might give Kristi some visual stimulus and would inspire in me some prose response.

One day, the phone rang. "Oh Mary, I love her poetry!" It was Kristi calling from Norway. "I started with *Oblique Prayers*," she said. That was the book I had started with. "And Mary, turn to page 14. 'I thought I was growing wings— it was a cocoon.'" I turned to page 14 and gasped to see that I had bracketed the same line. Then page 31. Then page 32. We had picked all the same lines. We laughed, even as our eyes welled up with tears, at the serendipity, the inspiration, of the process.

Then the next big hurdle—obtaining permission to use Levertov's words. I wrote to New Directions Publishing and told them of the proposed project as we imagined it at the time. Within three weeks we had a response. Yes, you can use any quote you want. No, you don't have to pay us anything.

We were stunned. The door had been flung open!

From then on, the phone lines between Iowa and Norway hummed as we brainstormed ideas. There were times when we fell into self-doubt, asking, "What are we doing?" or into despair, "How can we possibly communicate the greatness of this poetry?" Each time, Denise would answer our question.

For instance, one time I was wracked with questions about what right we had to take a line of her poetry and sail off with our own ideas. That night, as if by chance, I happened to read a footnote in *Breathing the Water.* In this footnote she explained what she was doing in her poems in that section of the book, poems based on someone else's poetry or art. She wrote, "A 'spinoff' then, is a verbal construct which neither describes nor comments but moves off at a tangent to, or parallel with, its inspiration." She was telling us, I have done with the work of others what you are doing with mine. Worry not.

That fall Kristi brought the paintings to Iowa, and we worked for weeks adding the prose words and tending to all the other details. Then one morning we transformed our basement into a gallery and stood back to look at what we had birthed. We started at the beginning, seeing and feeling, as if for the first time, the deep cultural, psychic and spiritual journey from innocence or apathy through the painful process of awakening and seeing the pain, the horror, the terror of the human condition. But the color and the words would not let us stay in this dark but necessary place. We moved through it step-by-step, painting-by-painting, coming finally to an awe so quiet, we didn't know when it began. We wept, thankful and honored that Denise's spirit trusted us and the Spirit empowered us to birth this project that evokes such transformation.

Nude Truths has been exhibited in galleries from coast to coast, touching many lives. Now, thanks to Brian McLaren and Deep Shift, it appears in book form. May the creative energy for transformative living, which moved through Levertov into Kristi and me and into this exhibit, now flow into you and through you into this wonderful, wounded world in which we live.

Mary Ylvisaker Nilsen

I in my balloon

light where the wind

permits a landing

DL

Is it innocence or ignorance, acceptance or apathy? Floating above humble earth—is that eternity or indifference? Only by landing, will we know.

1 My Balloon

"Is it innocence or ignorance, acceptance or apathy? Floating above humble earth—is that eternity or indifference? Only by landing will we know."

"I in my balloon light where the wind permits a landing," by Denise Levertov, from *Collected Earlier Poems 1940-1960,* copyright © 1957, 1958, 1959, 1960, 1961, 1979 by Denise Levertov, p. 116. Reprinted by permission of New Directions Publishing Corp.

2 The Illusion

"The child covers her eyes. Trouble vanishes. Adults cover their eyes. Troubles encroach, enlarge, entrench."

3 A Cocoon

"But how do we know a cocoon from within? From that safe place of half-light and half-life, of waiting and wondering? Only in the breaking open, in the flying free."

the key, now, to the next door,

the next terrors of freedom and joy

Freedom—breather of life into dry bones, granter of vision, empowering force—descends into the tyranny of choice, the burden of responsibility. And joy crumbles if clutched. Dare we open that door?

4 *Freedom and Joy*

"Freedom—breather of life into dry bones, granter of vision, empowering force—descends into the tyranny of choice, the burden of responsibility. And joy crumbles if clutched. Dare we open that door?"

"the key, now, to the next door, the next terrors of freedom and joy," by Denise Levertov, from *Oblique Prayers,* copyright © 1981, 1982, 1983, 1984 by Denise Levertov, p. 79. Reprinted by permission of New Directions Publishing Corp.

a candle, silently
melting beneath its flame,
seems to implore
attention, that it not burn its life
unseen

Daily, they die by the thousands—unnoticed, unnamed,
unaided—bone and flesh, sinew and soul. If we cannot save,
when we cannot help, our seeing gives their lives meaning.

5 A Candle

"Daily, they die by the thousands—unnoticed, unnamed, unaided—bone and flesh, sinew and soul. If we cannot save, when we cannot help, our seeing gives their lives meaning."

"a candle, silently melting beneath its flame, seems to implore attention, that it not burn its life unseen," by Denise Levertov from, *Oblique Prayers,* copyright © 1981, 1982, 1983, 1984 by Denise Levertov, p. 32. Reprinted by permission of New Directions Publishing Corp.

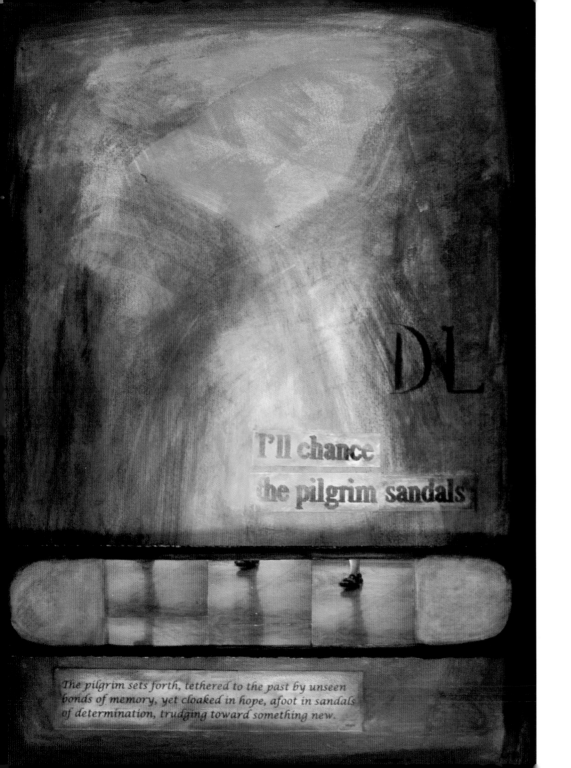

I'll chance
the pilgrim sandals

The pilgrim sets forth, tethered to the past by unseen
bonds of memory, yet cloaked in hope, afoot in sandals
of determination, trudging toward something new.

6 Pilgrim Sandals

"The pilgrim sets forth, tethered to the past by unseen bonds of memory, yet cloaked in hope, afoot in sandals of determination, trudging toward something new."

"I'll chance the pilgrim sandals," by Denise Levertov, from *A Door in the Hive,* copyright © 1989 by Denise Levertov, p. 6. Reprinted by permission of New Directions Publishing Corp.

No one confirms
an other unless
he himself rays forth
from a center

Imagine for a moment emotion—fierce, loving, true—finding
its way from your inscape to mine along smooth paths.
Try. For what we cannot imagine we cannot achieve.

7 Rays Forth

"Imagine for a moment emotion—fierce, loving, true—finding its way from your inscape to mine along smooth paths. Try. For what we cannot imagine we cannot achieve."

In each mind, even the most candid,

there are forests

Memories take root in our minds, innocently and automatically. Unexplored, unquestioned, unchallenged, they grow tall and dense, tangled and dangerous.

8 Forests

"Memories take root in our minds, innocently and automatically. Unexplored, unquestioned, unchallenged, they grow tall and dense, tangled and dangerous."

"In each mind, even the most candid, there are forests," by Denise Levertov, from *Sands of the Well,* copyright © 1994, 1995, 1996 by Denise Levertov, p. 12. Reprinted by permission of New Directions Publishing Corp.

9 Malicious Memory

"Descend. Risk the pain. Unearth the memory. Set it into your foundation as a solid building block. Then give it a name—past."

Malicious memory pulls downward with sudden force

Descend. Risk the pain. Unearth the memory. Set it into your foundation as a solid building block. Then give it a name—past.

-those foul

dollops of History

each day thrusts at us, pushing them

into our gullets-

Dead and wounded. Dead and starving. Truth and half-truths. Lies and counter-lies. The News: poison for our spirits, yet necessary for our communal soul.

10 Foul Dollops

"Dead and wounded. Dead and starving. Truth and half-truths. Lies and counter-lies. The News: poison for our spirits, yet necessary for our communal soul."

"those foul dollops of History each day thrusts at us, pushing them into our gullets," by Denise Levertov, from *Oblique Prayers,* copyright © 1981, 1982, 1983, 1984 by Denise Levertov, p. 35. Reprinted by permission of New Directions Publishing Corp.

Each day's terror, almost
a form of boredom

First it horrifies, then it tantalizes, then it dulls;
and we long for new horrors to jolt us back to life.
That is the terrifying terror of terror.

11 Day's Terror

"First it horrifies, then it tantalizes, then it dulls—and
we long for new horrors to jolt us back to life. That is
the terrifying terror of terror."

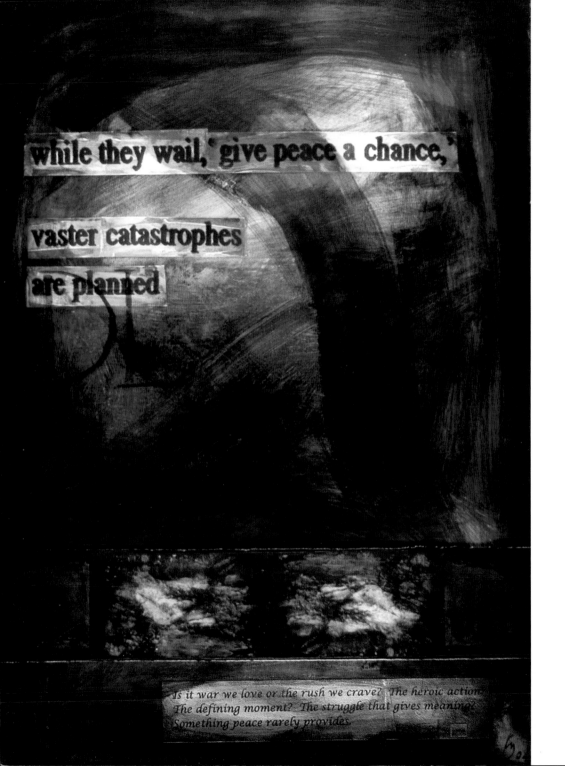

12 Catastrophes

"Is it war we love or the rush we crave? The heroic action? The defining moment? The struggle that gives meaning? Something peace rarely provides."

13 Plucking Truth

"When what we have believed lies shattered at our feet, we reach out for the idea, the image, the inspiration that comes from somewhere and changes everything. But we cannot pluck with clenched hand."

when roads of light and storm

open from darkness

Not what we wanted. Not the goal we sought while suffering through dark times. Must we say yes to light and storm, growth and pain? Will we?

14 Roads of Light

"Not what we wanted. Not the goal we sought while suffering through dark times. Must we say yes to light and storm, growth and pain? Will we?"

"when roads of light and storm open from darkness," by Denise Levertov, from *A Door in the Hive,* copyright © 1989 by Denise Levertov, p. 86. Reprinted by permission of New Directions Publishing Corp.

Through them alone

we keep our title, human,

word like an archway, a bridge, an altar

Without those named and unnamed great among us, the words humane and humanitarian could have frightful meanings. For without an image, we languish

15 *Our Title, Human*

"Without those named and unnamed great among us, the words humane and humanitarian could have frightful meanings. For without an image, we languish."

"Through them alone we keep our title, *human*, word like an archway, a bridge, an altar," by Denise Levertov, from *Oblique Prayers*, copyright © 1981, 1982, 1983, 1984 by Denise Levertov, p. 31. Reprinted by permission of New Directions Publishing Corp.

And the secret names

of all we meet who lead us deeper

into our labyrinth

The brooding Spirit works tirelessly, nudging us toward the voice, the word, the touch we need, then forcing the choice—to be attentive or to ignore.

16 Labyrinth

"The brooding Spirit works tirelessly, nudging us toward the voice, the word, the touch we need, then forcing the choice—to be attentive or to ignore."

great energy flowed from solitude,

and great power from communion

DL

Too long alone, the despondent toil. Too long together, the dutiful plod on.
By moving between solitude and communion, we discover a third way,
a way of great energy and great power.

17 Great Energy

"Too long alone, the despondent toil. Too long together, the dutiful plod on. By moving between solitude and communion, we discover a third way, a way of great energy and great power."

Peace, a presence,

an energy field more intense than war,

might pulse then

Peace pleads for redefinition: From non-violence to robust creativity. From the absence of war to the presence of compassion, cooperation, and collaboration.

18 Peace, a Presence

"Peace pleads for redefinition: From non-violence to robust creativity. From the absence of war to the presence of compassion, cooperation, and collaboration."

"Peace, a presence, an energy field more intense than war, might pulse then," by Denise Levertov, from *Breathing the Water,* copyright © 1987 by Denise Levertov, p. 40. Reprinted by permission of New Directions Publishing Corp.

when hope tried with a flutter of wings

DL

to lift me-

Dare I leave the safe ground of cynicism? The security of despair? Dare I risk believing the world could be different? That I could change?

19 Hope Tried

"Dare I leave the safe ground of cynicism? The security of despair? Dare I risk believing the world could be different? That I could change?"

"when hope tried with a flutter of wings to lift me," by Denise Levertov, from *A Door in the Hive,* copyright © 1989 by Denise Levertov, p. 102. Reprinted by permission of New Directions Publishing Corp.

Yet our hope lies

in the unknown,

in our unknowing

To move beyond our wearied "Why?" and hope for answers, signs, even miracles is easy. But to hope in? In what? In whom? Herein lies the invitation.

20 Our Unknowing

"To move beyond our wearied 'Why?' and hope for answers, signs, even miracles is easy. But to hope in? In what? In whom? Herein lies the invitation."

"Yet our hope lies in the unknown, in our unknowing," by Denise Levertov, from *Candles in Babylon,* copyright © 1982 by Denise Levertov, p. 109. Reprinted by permission of New Directions Publishing Corp.

21 *Needful Journey*

"We cry out for a guide. Who can travel the distance without one? We long for companions. Who will come? Made bold by promise and memory, we set forth."

"the needful journey, the veiled distance, imperative mystery," by Denise Levertov, from *A Door in the Hive,* copyright © 1989 by Denise Levertov, p. 3. Reprinted by permission of New Directions Publishing Corp.

the mystery

that there is anything, anything at all,

let alone cosmos, joy, memory, everything,

rather than void

Not often, just now and then, a thought interrupts, clarifying
our perspective—all this might just as easily not have been. But—
I am! We are! Everything is! In this mystery we live. Sustained.

22 The Mystery

"Not often, just now and then, a thought interrupts, clarifying our perspective—all this might just as easily not have been. But—I am! We are! Everything is! In this mystery we live. Sustained."

drawing us from tree to tree

towards the time and the unknown place

where we shall know

what it is to arrive

DL

In moments when scales fall like dying leaves from our eyes and we allow
ourselves to be shaken by beauty, humbled with gratitude, and released into joy,
eternity is ours.

23 Drawing Us

"In moments when scales fall like dying leaves from our eyes and we allow ourselves to be shaken by beauty, humbled with gratitude, and released into joy, eternity is ours."

"drawing us from tree to tree towards the time and the unknown place where we shall know what it is to arrive," by Denise Levertov, from *Breathing the Water,* copyright © 1987 by Denise Levertov, p. 51. Reprinted by permission of New Directions Publishing Corp.

24 An Awe

"An awe so quiet I don't know when it began," by Denise Levertov, from *Oblique Prayers,* copyright © 1981, 1982, 1983, 1984 by Denise Levertov, p. 85. Reprinted by permission of New Directions Publishing Corp.

Stream Poems

Emotions kindle emotions, ideas generate ideas, creativity sparks creativity. Ignite your creative energy by picking a particular phrase from a painting that inspires you, haunts you, captures your mind or heart. Begin with that line and then spin off, letting your own ideas flow.

One way to do this is to start each line of a poem with the last word of the preceeding line or a form of the last word. For instance, you might pick the line, "Each day's terror," and then go on with the lines, "terror in the streets / streets filled with children…"

Or maybe you pick the line, "An awe so quiet," your next line might be, "quietness that seeps into my soul / a soul yearning for peace…"

Or just write as the Spirit moves.

Impressionistic Art

Try igniting your creative energy by picking a phrase from the exhibit and opening your imagination to color and form.

Draw or paint your reaction to the images contained in the words.

Consider repeating this spin-off creativity from time to time. Note how your responses change and deepen.